a generation
30 years of poetry

sheryl massaro

ISBN: 979-8-9887537-2-8 (Paperback)

LCCN: 2023920328

Front cover image by Sheryl Massaro
Book design by Sheryl Massaro
Font used throughout is Helvetica

Printed by DiggyPOD, Inc., Tecumseh, MI, USA

First printing edition 2023

Sheryl Massaro
FAC Artist Studios
7 North Market St., Suite 25
Frederick MD 21701
www.sherylmassaro.com

*poems from
the 2nd generation of my life*

with thanks to

The Raw Art Review, Fall 2019,
for publishing *Blue Peril*
and awarding it Honorable Mention in
The 2020 Charles Bukowski Prize for Poetry

Honeyguide Literary Magazine, October 2020
for publishing *Rain Forest*

Free State: A Harvest of Maryland Poets, 1989,
for publishiing *The Death of Trees*

contents

artwork

images of oil paintings by sheryl massaro:

cover   *comus road*

early   *early bird gets the pomegranate*

ripening   *no prejudice among pears*

at last   *pollen*

early

Early Bird Gets the Pomegranate, Sheryl Massaro ©

100ºf

so this is when goldie flies
from my father's head out the window.
it is when my mother grabs the bird cage
and hangs it on the shed.
goldie! we yell. She's there, way off
in the top of a pine,
bright, scared, faint.

some day, well after blue boy,
her beau, has passed on,
she will stop talking
to the budgie in the mirror.
around the house she will fly
and into a wall and die soon after.

at times i feel i am waiting for her still
in that first summer shower
that came through bright sunlight.
she had flown back among the sprinkles
then, and tottered on her perch
drinking for a long time
from her little plastic cup.

early

somewhere between the front page
and the last comes the weather,
tossing fronts to the stratosphere,
letting them fall where they may.

between the highs and colds
and lows and warms
comes a lull of nothing.
a little coolness,
a lot of stillness,
rest.

whiffs of coffee
drift into the world,
and a faint pop of toasters,
a shaky scraping of chair legs,

assuring that beginnings
are beginning again today,
unperturbed
that today will have an end.

evocation

it could have been a dream,
the honeysuckle and snow
spraying together
through the window.
it could have been
another's hair, white
and bent as frozen twigs,
or another's eyes,
lucid and quick
as spring streams.
yet it was my world
and face i woke to
before one morning
had composed itself.
a glimpse of seasons
tangled in their sleep,
of youth and aging caught
in their secret bed.
it could have been a dream,
except for the gasp and scramble
of time to right itself.
i could have gone blinking
on with the day, but waited,
watching the sun's rising,
wondering what compels
the universe
to hide its play.

loam

in the longer days,
the beds forget their dark pasts
of clay and stone as roots
ease through worm-sifted soil.
green things wake like bears
from winter, hungry for air
and light and a good washing,
old friends now, groggily
commiserating as they levitate
from earth's heart
to its shaggy skin.

this is the time of the new,
when humans gaze quietly
at a beautiful, beautiful thing
and grow tingly at the thought
of its softness, fragility.
soon comes the butterfly,
more delicate still, woozy
in its trajectory, yet finding
every early purply something.
yes, insect, we survived
another winter and now
let's rest among
those tender blooms
in their deep loam.

green is the age

green is the age of all children,
say the italians. not ripe, but
starting to soften. still hanging
from, onto, something grounded.

a dry, silvery green of olive groves,
an ancient green of boreal woods,
a papery green of vineyards,
a fickle green of lindens

turning to the blazing sun
of adolescence, the new green
of a young tomato that ripens
to the blood red
                of a woman
in her prime, or to the plum
bruising on the arms
of the elderly.

we true bugs

which among the orders of spineless
beings cherishes its thorax, abdomen,
head, spindly legs, and iridescent
or sadly drab encasing? are any
conscious of whether their mouths face
down or forward, sucking or chewing?
should the stink bug be commended
for its single-minded destruction,
the bed bug for its blood thirst,
the cicada for its frenzy?
life can be hard for these hard
little beings, these technically
true, nimble bugs whose numbers
overwhelm us lumbering bipeds

who offer poison, soap suds, squishing.

i doubt they have a clue
where they stand along the precarious,
quivering filaments of the food web,
or even if they suck flora or blood
or themselves are prey. like us.

pearly things

so many pearly things in life,
all a bit surreal. there is

the pearl itself, from a troubled bed
of grit and nacre. an opaque gem,
a bland and lovely face.

teeth can be pearly glints
when lips part in evening light.

the frosted land beyond
our winter door, a snow pearl.

a baby's skin, dark or light,
a pearl made flesh. magic.

the cold, old, dead moon
seems more benign
when we imagine it a pearl.

and, in deepest africa,
forever there has lived
a pearly white spider
spinning its black web.

the canoe in the trees

you might have sailed
an ancient flood
to find your first home
high among the trees.

you might have yearned
to be a mighty trunk
again, riding the wild
currents of air.

when i climb to reach you
in your crook of a bough,
will i find the skeleton
of an antideluvian,
or will your hull
be empty, open
to any fiction?

you might agree
to return with me
to the rivers, or i might
shimmy down alone
as you stay aloft,
paddles stowed,
gathering snow.

roost

what a crow this night is,
no moon, no stars. close
and dark and everywhere,
silent in the absent color
of the pines.

they say *two crows for joy*,
and here they come with evening.
hundreds spread, stream
across the sunset,
filled with the yearning
to breed and breed.

then there are more,
and more come,
still as stones
in the ancient roost,
waiting for all of the shadows
to find their places.

the rites of morning

in this mind of mine
i am dressed, sneakers tied,
if not eager to place one foot
before the other then sure
i will become so
after the first fifty steps
of my journey
to the house of coffee,
or just around the block
to get the juices flowing.

but first, i pee
and take a pill

and then i make
my home coffee

and then i raise the shades
on the patio door,

on the kitchen windows,

on the right front windows,

then i venture out
until i reach the paper

and while i'm at it
i fetch from the mail box
ads   bills   catalogs
pleas for money:
for sick children
for starving children

the sick chesapeake
political anything   the heart
cancer   sad veterans
war   peace   tibet

and i take this world
back inside and raise
the final shades,

the ones in the left front room

and i and the hummingbird,
who has fed in privacy
at the window box,
hover in place
on our sides
of the pane.

cub scout

little bird voice chattering
at me as i cross the road
would i like to buy some popcorn
sure when i'm done shopping
a mini hand shook mine

i meant it! incredulous!
we have caramel and kettle
and butter and a few sweet
pretzels and just kernels
you cook on the stove my dad
likes these and i grab a box
of butter *keep the change*

silence   another mini hand
and a hug! oh my he's so grateful
never had a little one hug
my barren middle   o tenderness

live long sweetheart
no war for you please
no harm

other people's

one foot led another
along the linoleum,
passed the makeshift rooms
of consignments.

too stodgy, too tacky, still a thing?
bakelite. the woodwork, amazing.
the pottery, leaden.
i can use that frame
and that mirror, find
new clothes for that sofa
new wires to that lamp.

like rescued pets
they came home to live with me
in the days before i grew wary
of haunted objects, the items
of others. things sat on, looked in
things that had lit and witnessed,
things drunk from, walked on,
objects of adornment.

this i remember
as i ponder you, human,
whom i want to love,
want to take home,
but pause at the thought
of others in your memory.
of whether I can be kind
to their ghosts, and you to mine.

the dreaming

angel, what aboriginal
story are you from,
for you are not a spirit
i recognize from any
civilization.

if i could touch
your many wings,
or the circle of your brain
or belly, i might begin
to know your story,

but you hover
just beyond my reach
like a dream
i can almost remember
as i wake,
but not quite.

the hood of evening

he finds a seat in the corner
in the back on the train home
and slouches down
down down in the seat.

and as he slips into
the hidden world of sleep,

his jacket rides up
and the hood bunches
in the crook of his neck.

the heavy earth turns slowly
as the train rolls on from day's light,

and the old earth hunches
into its deep hood of evening

seeking rest from another
bright, demanding day.

the dove

a dove alit on
the fretwork of rails
in the train yard,
an odd paleness
among the grime,
a softening of steel.

a working dove,
laboring at peace,
uplifting those
off to jobs, those
coming home,
those without.

a dove that never
goes south for winter,
never abandons its post.
it is like a mother that way,

whom you remember
as you ride off.

if days

if days were people,
would they roll down
grassy hills in play,
splash in the creek,
get lost in a book,
work in daylight,
sleep in darkness,
softly belch before bedtime?
would they live themselves
to the fullest? would they
look like round watch faces
and count themselves down?
if people were days
would they go before
or follow and never meet?
be remembered
for their weather,
for being made the most of
or having been wasted?
would they have
a day of birth and one of death?
would we have tumbled
onto earth together
yawing like a tired comet,
we people and our days,
from foggy pre-eternity,
and will we tumble off?

ripening

No Prejudice Among Pears, Sheryl Massaro ©

the milliner

i expected his hands
to be different, maybe
a bit more matter of fact,
but the hat i now wore
had appeared from above
and been tenderly fitted.
with just a fingertip or two
he deftly moved my head
to one side a bit,
then to the other.
i barely felt a lightness
as suddenly he lifted the hat
from my head, then
replaced it at an angle.
rakish.

as if on cue,
my thoughts beneath it
raced on the bias
to crooked pros
and twisted cons,
to logic canted
just enough to burst
like fireworks, thudding
quietly, arcing in splendor,
then crackling
and falling
and gone
in a puff,
smoke.

i'll take it, i said.

the common fig

a rabbi says that YHWH
is the dyslexic's name for God,
which should be HWHY
and mean the He/She,
the terms for sexes
being less disparate
in ancient times,

almost less important,

almost interchangeable,

one sex taking on
the tasks of the other
as the needs arose,

whatever it took
to keep creation going.

like the common fig,

a compelling fruit
whose single sac
of boy and girl florets
form undisturbed,
grow sweet, complex
in the diminutive,
rosy universe
we break open
to savor.

koi pond

a place of peace
for red-gold beauties
to meander
from one bank
to another, or simply
to meet in the middle

until my stone skipped
twice across the surface,
then sank.

       no koi were hit,
but double rings of ripples
roiled their placid world,
each ring an unexpected wave
in tideless waters.

in dappled light
the golden koi still shimmer,
but in fear.

blue peril

what came in an instant was how
my young friends and i were stopped
by the local tough girls on the towpath
behind the post office. there were only
two of them—sue somebody
and someone else's big sister.
both were big, in high school.
sue took a liking to me,
who had my mother's scarf
with the map of florida on it
tied around my head. sue untied it.
there were rollers in my hair (pink sponge).
sue liked that. i was terrified.
as she put the scarf back on i tensed
my throat and neck so i couldn't be strangled.
she tied it so gently
i felt ashamed. they made us walk
a little way with them.
a guy in a truck drove by
and they were gone.

then i was in high school, missing the bus,
walking home alone. i could see all the way
down the shortcut, so i took it.
i didn't worry about the boys
coming the other way because i knew
by the time we passed it would be
in a clearing, by houses. the boys
were speaking softly, and gave
some sort of greeting.
i was beginning to answer
when one moved a hand
between my legs. it was almost polite.

i brushed it away, puzzled at my own grace.
if they looked back, they didn't see my face.
and then i remembered hearing
about a local pregnant woman
who had had four miscarriages
and was raped by some men
who tried her door one night
and found it unlocked.
look away, they said, not wanting her
to know them, *this won't hurt you*.
it didn't when it should have,
and that baby lived.

all this came back when i lifted the hood
of *blue peril*, my car, to see gone
what i already knew was gone—the battery.
one notes how correctly some things
are stolen, how carefully the cables
had been unfastened and set aside.
nothing cut, nothing else touched.
quiet thieves in a parking lot,
taking and not taking much.

taming the littles

come here, little things that fret
my heart, come into my blood.
let me warm you, we'll talk.

past is passed,
there is no need to yell.
i would introduce you recent arrivals
to those i've known too long,
but then you would learn from them,
and i like you young and ignorant.

now me, i live to learn.
i have learned to insult you,
more subtly, more unpredictably
than any one of you
has ever flattened me.
but together, my littles,
you are a force.
silly, mangy, yet a force.

come look at you and me
together in the mirror.
you never dreamed
you are so invisible.
speaking of dreaming,
you have become way too vain
as metaphors. my blood
may lend you a home,
but my dreams are blessed.
you, who know no rest,
cannot join me there.
but on the coverlet you wait,
like little dogs ready to pounce.
as day turns the dark drapes

pale and filmy, you lick your chops.
it's a deft maneuver i've perfected—
a graceful billowing of the bed clothes
and off you scatter,
turtles on your backs.

squirm though you may, dears,
you are invisible.
shush. sit.

late may

she remembered wondering
what sort of ludicrous landscape
would be home for the fat bee by her head
and how light the screen door was,
how tired its small noise was becoming.
the baggy wire net, the fibers spreading
instead of frayed where the kids poked
their fingers through. the sun so bright
she couldn't see well inside. she thought
it was the dog knocking groceries
from her arms. and then to feel her drunk
husband's palm, oddly soft as it struck her and
hauled its hard knuckles back,
again and again.

she landed by a window
under the iris heads. the dizzy bee.
the blue petals, their veins deeper
than those inside an eyelid.
the screen door made its double,
muffled bang. slim leaves rose
and drooped sharply,
                              the way
a little girl's hands dangle
as she walks as fast as she can
to get to the other side.

ghosts

we all should go home in mango season,
when the sweet reddening paisleys
dangle like sexual somethings
and the bark glistens like braids
and the feet of everyone
are equally wet.

but we go home in an indian autumn,
when the dry sky is too blue to be
believed, home to whitening parents
who touch the lines in our own skin.
we lounge on the verandas
of old mansions full of monkeys,

leaving the salons behind us
to the long dead, whose
beautiful perfumes still come,
with a faint ring of bangles,
as if a great party goes on.

a history

many years ago, on a farm
in southern germany,
a massive straw mattress
filled a very old carved bed.
it was wide enough to hold
a family and their body heat
under the eider covers
on frigid winter nights.
this particular winter,
a pretty, young teen
slept between her mother
and new stepfather.
the mother slept soundly
on one side of the bed,
and the man seduced the girl
on the other.

one day, the mother noticed
daylight was lasting longer,
the sky was bluer, the ice
in the animals' trough
was more brittle,
and her daughter seemed
to be with child. the truth
tumbled out, and the girl
was given heavy barrels to move
up hills, over fields, anywhere,
everywhere until these labors
caused her to miscarry.

much later, in a new century,
the grown girl emigrated,
married, had daughters.

when one daughter's children
were grown, and she
and their father had retired,
the couple were asked
to adopt a little dog.
the sweet pup became
their last child, their last
baby, until the woman,
who had seemed to be
well through her change of life,
realized she was pregnant.
her doctors knew her body
would not survive carrying
this child, and she knew,
and her husband knew.
she endured a procedure
not unusual for women
of a certain age, and her last
true child was mourned.

so many ways to gauge
the worth of lives,
and none of us is God.

pulse, orlando

squeeze the dense rubber rod
the nurse nestled in your palm
and gently curled your fingers
around. up pumps the good vein
in the good arm,
                          and the sterile
metal nib pierces yet again
the small field of tiny scars.
decades, it has been,

giving fluid life in lieu of children,
gallons of universal blood.

now, when our prayers
are not enough and our actions
are weighted in mourning,
it flows and overflows,

this need to give, to give life
when lives are taken.

hours, it has been, waiting in line
for city blocks, to give more life
to those whose lives are leaving.

for decades, we would wait to give.
we will need forever.

terrain

how many of earth's coverings
have you crossed to be here,
where you stand in a late sun
on a late day in summer?
how many ruts has your wagon cut
in the grasses, how many waves
has your boat stirred in its wakes?
how much skin have you pierced
to reach how much tissue and bone?
how much have you laid open,
having taken, and not known how to close?

these things i ask me in the soft lowlands
with my back warm in the ancient,
golden sun. even the occasional car
passes in quiet. this moment in an old land,
mine to take and think, *i must try,*
when the moment moves forward,
i must try to be gentle.

crows

this is not a day to study
the complexities of crows—
not with the leaves going hard,
the sun barely sustaining its pull,
the pond dying. fertility has grown
exhausted after its amazing climb
to autumn.

this is a day just to rest
on that mesa and wonder
how a crow absorbs the spectrum
and finds the plumpest worm
and soars with the weight of both.

chestnuts

i try to imagine a picnic beneath
an american chestnut tree.
not one of the gene-spliced,
blight-resistant saplings
we design to grow now, but a tree
that shot straight and tall
before the fatal blight. one that canopied
100 feet high, with a girth to dwarf humans.
one whose wood was light and hard
and rarely rotted. whose seeds
filled rail cars, destined for roasting
on cold city corners.

i try to imagine our sorrow
at the loss, yet another genocide
in an age of them. four billion trees
gone from two hundred million acres.
i imagine a picnic in woods full
of old growth.
                    chestnuts crazed,
flexing with strength. i imagine
how far and deep the old roots
have spread, unharmed from the blight
that stunts the still-struggling saplings.
how far and deep and entwined with roots
of the beech, the oak, the maple,
now free to grow in the sun
once hidden
by the crowded canopy
of chestnut.

under balance rock

the corners of five states meet
just below the top of a mountain
bordering tennessee and georgia.
we learn this after climbing up
for the sake of looking down—
one of the peculiar enigmas of distance.
at 25,000 feet in the plane to get here,
for example, one felt free from the snow
on the farms. at 37,000, it was black pines
on the mountains we were delivered from.

then we pilgrims stopped looking down.
the horizon had disappeared at that height.
we began to sleep, fearless yet so far
from earth, just as some are napping
here now, near the top of a mountain,
in the shadow of an eleven-hundred ton
rock balanced by a far smaller one.

one by one we wake,
softly discussing the view,
where we came from,
the perfect weather,
how the veins on the belly of the big rock are so
like the red clay below.

we feel guarded here,
protected from thoughts
of leaving for journeys beyond
or back to places
where there is little evidence
we ever left, we who have travelled

far and high and together
to learn how small a thing it can be
that keeps a world from falling.

night ward

a peculiar healing
happens in the night—
consciousness dreaming
itself clean, cells renewing
themselves throughout
the brilliant body
that is its own home
and its own child departing.

and when the healing is done,
the senses wake to stretch,
to piss, to sniff
the freshened molecules of earth
just waking to light,
its white nurse,
her dry hands,
her wing of morning.

the arm

i used to wonder how many heads
had slept in that arm's crook,
what shades of hair, their lengths,
frizzy, wavy, straight. did they
face in the morning or evening
or whenever or did they spoon
or did they side-by-side,
backs of hands just touching
while sweat dried. i wondered
if they spent their days
doing useful things, or did
one just basically wait
for the other's tender attention
and the other for aching need.
did they keep a neat house
or were dishes too often in the sink
or was it a kind of old-hippie
house with interesting, creative
doodads, a mobile somewhere.
not often, but i did wonder.

we spoke in a dream last night,
had many conversations.

i woke thinking yes, this is how
we can progress, gradually.
but then i had my coffee
and remembered it has been
decades, and it is no more.

at last

Pollen, Sheryl Massaro ©

dusk

the tractor stops. its rumble
disintegrates into muffled quiet.
even though the farm seems
very still, corn rustles
as if enjoying conversing.
it sounds like many turning pages
of a story for children abed.

sheep listen
as they rip the rich grasses
and chomp thoughtfully.
pretty good story, they agree
and follow the lead rump down a hill.

i sit high up on the machine in this world
of singular sounds that are not language,
yet tell me things. the barn inhales
and exhales, a hawk yearns and cries
for distant prey. a cow lows,

and i confuse it with a whale
singing deep as another day closes.
as the moon comes,
so does a wolf's moaning,
old, remote.

sounds

we are heading into summer,
yet a hard, spotted leaf falls
now and then from the photinias

i've let grow huge and sick.
you'd think it was autumn,
or the closing down of rivendell

as the elves depart. In a breeze,
the leaves tap the patio

more insistently as the tree-bushes
clamor feed us, dose us, woman!

yet still I sit in the sparse shade
they offer me

and write this poem.

autumn

there is something
about old stone houses
in autumn, something
about crumbly mortar,

and washes of golden light
on passive stone that one knows

has many stories at hand
in its crystalline structure,
old memories of earth before

seasons as we know them
existed, perhaps.

there is magic in the leaves
reddening, goldening,
riding the currents down
to earth. it all is so

comfortable, like old folks
at peace in a well-run
nursing home. their luster
and tenderness stay with you

all the way home.

oaks, aspens, firs

they seem content
in their alignment
on the mountainside.
birds might take seeds
from the realm of red oak
to the horizon of golden aspen,
but few seeds will take root,
as will few from the fir cones
tumbling down the slopes.

temperatures, soil conditions
keep each species where it grows best.
a breathtaking sight, oddly orderly,

especially in autumn when it seems
the oaks catch fire and the aspens
shimmer in the heat and the firs
douse the mountainside in darkness.

then all grow quiet under snow.

the quiet season

at the edge of the pueblo,
someone always listens
to this water. anyone
fleeing a spat
or yet another sharp blue sky
or the darkness inside
or tourists
or dust.

dogs drink it,
then scuffle on the banks
for territory.
                it rinses skin
and clothing (the skin of skin)
and blood. it sends yellow leaves
and urine on their ways.

it shows the sun and moon
their faces, and us ours, always.

this water
never takes a breath
in its conversation,

even in the quiet season.
even when its own skin hardens
in the cold,
                it erodes
from the gurgles beneath.

a night at the folger

nearly 40 years since you came
from backstage with other poets
and held my eyes that held back
in the wonderment that you
remembered (even that you knew)
how i had opened
as you had taken my hand
and drawn me in a year before.

you knew these things.
you took them with you
as i turned from your
pending cloud bank.
must keep my *self*, i thought,
which would have gone blind
in those clouds.

yet at times you are here
when i wake. and i wonder
what your afterlife has been.
i wonder if your ruined body
is whole again. if your ardor
has sweetened, ceded
its grasp for conquest.

if in my afterlife
your eyes and mine will hold,
or if still you will be playing
with your words.

in time

we will have met
too old to have babies,
and so we will create
invisible things
time together,
the memories of it.

we will be there
for friends, and anyone.
we will give our smiles
and words. money.

we will feel pain
and we will have fear,
and remember that we
have endured these before.

we will be there
and then we won't be,
or will be, but invisible.

the death of trees

the earth will be lighter
when the redwoods are gone.
the biggest trees of the universe
are dying from stress, from straining,
from wounds, from a sick branch
pruned flush with its trunk,
from confining intruding pathogens
until the good pulp is pushed
to the outmost limits—from starving,
from the heartwood rotting.

my grandmother would swim far into
the heart of lake erie until our mother
could barely see her pale arms stroking
like tiny white leaves lost at sea.

we stroked our mother's arms
and legs and forehead as she waned
in our last gift of a peaceful death.

our father's seeping limbs were gauzed
and so we held his ancient head
as he drifted to his angel wife

and brothers and mother and father
and buddies from work and the war

and left us here, the barren offspring,
and then we will be gone.

calais

you study our starvation in bronze
and ponder the technique, the genius
of rodin, touch the patina sizzling
in california light.

you study our hollows and wonder
at the resolve of six burghers martyring
to end the siege of their calais.
that was long ago, and still we walk
in the world *paris, london, copenhagen*
wondering how other copies,
our other selves, are faring.
morlanwelz, basel

you and the world circle us slowly
philadelphia, washington, tokyo
surreptitiously touching our sinews,
bones, jaws. *pasadena, new york*
this is what it means to serve a people.
let our ears, lips, sunken eyes
feel your fingertips. *oslo, seoul*

the laundry

a line is strung
as they do in europe,
and laundry ripples
like prayer flags
across a kitchen
whose outside wall
has been blown open.

from a distance,
the whole building
gapes like charred
dollhouses, glistens
from glass shards
in every window, mirror.

some come, small figures,
up the backbone of stairs
to touch what home is left,
sit in remaining chairs
at tables still standing.

a cup of steaming coffee
appears from memory,
and the morning routine,
and the sleep left behind
in the sheets.
                    good talks
linger here in the ruins,
with aromas, good meals.
the sun comes through
unobstructed now,
and the breezes, the view.

as if after a long night
of carousal, it is very quiet,
very contemplative, perplexing.
a good time to fold laundry.

a dream

the dream was of
a terribly sad friend
who was offered
a solo trip to space
on a craft that could
self-destruct. if
our friend landed on
the moon and chose
to push that button,
from earth we would
see the flare
and lift our prayers.
if no flare,
we would wave
as the moon rose.
we waved for many moons.
then we prayed.

the selective wasting of time

at the wrought iron table,
under its umbrella, my feet
on the rungs, sometimes

i smell the vape shop
or hear martial arts calls
from the other side
of the fence, but then

they dissipate as the breeze
comes through as it always does

out back, and the firm leaves
of photinia faintly clap,

the ferns of bolted asparagus
wave like coral in a tide,

the rose scents, the wind chimes
ting, and ting again,

and i think about time

and wonder what it does
with its time.

time

it begins with sand
in an hourglass so large
with a waist so small
it takes years, years
for all the grains to fall.

one by one,
or a few together,
the first sands cascade
along the filaments
of gravity onto the soft
arcs of the bottom globe

into the unknown
toward the unknowable.
the brave, tiny grains
never look back.
the grains like sheep
look ahead ahead ahead
and maybe to the side

as they travel
in a leaderless herd
to sweet rest
at the bottom
of their world

or the top.

hearing, the last to go

in my young time i think i remember
there was no frown on my face.
i would smile straight at the one
in the mirror. now, i dare a glance
sidelong, then away.

i believe my hands
would reach out and hold others,
but now they stay close, closed.

they will not accept the orange
your hands want to share,
but my tongue waters.

what i carve in steam
on the bath mirror clears.
so are the sounds of your mouth.
meaningful, then meaning
drips away.

at last

why can't i just go, he asked,
the old man with the strongest will to live
she'd ever encountered, the geriatrician,
until yesterday when the white blood cells
began the wrong trajectory.

he'd been working with them, soldiering on
as they fought for him. she'd stop by late
each night, and he'd ask how
the numbers looked today. they looked ok
for several weeks and then began to waver,
and then they wavered more,
and when he asked one night
she smiled and held his hand.
maybe she held his hand.
i imagine it, and believe it.

when i came in the morning,
his hands were curled, as if
someone had held them as he left.
i understand that is one of the body's
odd responses after death,
but i like to think his doctor
had held his hands until his angel
wife held them, and then i held them
and my brother
kissed his forehead.

an afternoon

84 is where her breath
stopped after 30 hours
of the body's organs
and systems ticking down
in their instinctive order
in the subdued light
of the sterile room
where we waited,
drifting with her
until the edge
so that she need not
go alone

heaven

there is a place
where we are perfectly lovely
in our happiness.
where old parents embrace
in their youth with a love
they hold as memory now,
where our old dogs run to us
again with a courage and grace
that startle them and us into joy.
where butterflies rest on our shoulders
and sing with the voices
we do not yet know they have.
where our children are always in our arms,
their silken heads always at our cheek.
where we hold children we did not know
we have. we hold them all now,
in this place where we rest our own heads
in the arms of angels, where our angels rest in
the hands of God. even now—
as we scrape the carrots, brush the hair, empty
the trash, iron, walk, work—
our heaven is beside us and in us and is us,
our perfect roundness of love, our place.

what is beautiful

why do we know that the grass
between our toes is soft or even green,
and why do we think green and soft
are nice things for grass to be,
and how do we know what *nice* is or that water,
when liquid, is delicate as it flows through our
fingers yet can break them
when chilled and how is it that we know
the difference and know that knowing
makes a difference even though
the knowing is invisible and grass
and sky and water and you and i are not
. . . or are we? eventually we will be,
and then how will we know anything
about anything or will nothing matter
or will everything matter
and with what will we determine this—
a sense, an organ, or with the hitherto
unrecognizable something with which
i sense the ongoing joys
of the dead and gone,
with which i see,
with something other than sight,
utter beauty.

sky

the clouds have changed today.
still heavy with the greys

of many days of april rain, yes,
but some hold a light i'd forgotten.

they keep moving, as clouds do,
and soon one grows so thin
it splits like an amoeba,

parting tips growing wispier
and yellow. (i'd forgotten yellow.)
soon, they barely touch

and i think of michelangelo's
God reaching that forefinger
out to adam's for the spark of life,
or just the gift of blue sky.

Sheryl Massaro is an oil painter, poet, and photographer based in Frederick, MD. She holds an MFA in Creative Writing/Poetry from The American University and studied with several key poets, including Allen Ginsberg, Stanley Kunitz, W.S. Merwin, et al. Her other books include *duino elegies, rainer maria rilke—an interpretive translation*, and a collection of her own work, *afloat—a raft of water poems.*

Massaro's visual art and poetry, though often based on the recognizable, share a deeper, "off to the side" look at life than the purely representational. In each of these arts, she taps into and conveys life's undertow—the unspoken, unseen energy that binds artists and their readers or viewers.

For information on Massaro's books and art, please visit sherylmassaro.com.